PETERBOROU

A Portrait in Old Picture Postcards

£3

by
June and Vernon Bull

S.B. Publications
1988

First published in 1988 by S.B. Publications

5 Queen Margaret's Road, Loggerheads, Nr. Market Drayton, Shropshire, TF9 4EP.

Reprinted 1989

© Copyright S.B. Publications 1988.

ISBN 1 870708 07 5

Printed and bound in Great Britain by Witley Press Ltd., Hunstanton, Norfolk, PE36 6AD.

CONTENTS

CONTENTS CONTINUED

CONTENTS CONTINUED

ACKNOWLEDGEMENTS

The authors are indebted to the following people without whose help this book would not have been possible:

Stephen Perry for loaning the postcards used on pages 16, 17, 18, 39 and 54.
Roy Sturgess of the Peterborough Postcard Society.
Jack Gaunt.
The late Harry Miles.
Steve Benz: editorial and marketing.

Also published by S.B. Publications in the series 'A Portrait in Old Picture Postcards'.

Bootle	Chester	Liverpool
Bootle, Volume 2	Chester, Volume 2	The Black Country
Bridgnorth	Chesterfield	Norwich
	Chirk and the Glyn Valley Tramway	Shrewsbury

INTRODUCTION

Peterborough owes its origin to a monastery founded in 655 A.D. by Paeda, King of Mercia. Over the centuries the town developed around the monastery, which became the present Cathedral, and up until the early 19th century, it was still a small Fenland market town.

The first sign of any real expansion was when the Great Northern Railway established their works at New England, a village north of Peterborough, in 1853. On 17th March, 1874, a public meeting was held in a packed Drill Hall giving details of a new Charter granted by Queen Victoria. The Charter detailed the amalgamation of a number of parishes which were to be split into three wards: South Ward — south of the River Nene; East Ward — St. John's Parish, east of the railway, and part of St. Mary's Parish; North Ward — St. John's Parish, west of the railway, and parts of St. Paul's and St. Mark's Parishes including Dogsthorpe and Lincoln Road.

The city continued to grow in all directions, which instigated a proposal in 1921 to extend the boundaries to include Gunthorpe, Paston, Werrington, Walton, Fletton, Stanground and Longthorpe. This became the Peterborough Extension Order (1928), which was implemented on 1st April, 1929.

In 1967, the Government decided that Peterborough should help to relieve some of London's housing problems. The proposal led to the inception of the Peterborough Development Corporation in 1968. The city continues to expand even though the Development Corporation has been disbanded.

The city has seen numerous changes over the years, especially the opening of the massive and prestigious Queensgate Shopping Centre on 9th March, 1982, built in the city centre at a cost of £35 million with a further £30 million spent on the fitting out of the stores and shops.

The purpose of this book is to show how much the city has changed since the beginning of this century and illustrating these changes with old and rare picture postcards.

Prior to 1902, the correspondence on a postcard had to be shared with the illustration on the front. These early small postcards were known as 'Court Cards'. In 1902, new Post Office regulations permitted a larger size, which we use today, and also allowed the correspondence to be written on the reverse of the postcard. Gradually over the years, postcard collecting became a national craze and postcard albums could be found in a prominent position in almost every home.

Millions of postcards were posted annually encouraged by the cheap ½d postage rate and the vast choice of cards published, depicting every subject imaginable. This era was known as the Golden Age of Postcards. The hobby remained extremely popular until the end of the First World War, after which it went into a gradual decline, caused mainly by rises in postage rates and the increased use of the telephone. Many collections remained dormant or were forgotten, until collectors began to rediscover and appreciate these treasures of a bygone age.

The sequence of postcards have been selected to follow a nostalgic tour of the city and its surrounding villages. The tour commences at Alwalton, through Longthorpe village, along Thorpe Road, across the Crescent Bridge and into the city centre and the Cathedral Precincts, then proceeding into Broadway, New Road, Eastfield Road and Newark village. The tour then follows a south to north route commencing at Stanground and Fletton, up London Road to Town Bridge, along Broad Bridge Street and back into Market Place. Along Long Causeway and Westgate with excursions up Park Road, Gladstone Street and Cromwell Road. The tour concludes with visits to Lincoln Road, Millfield, Dogsthorpe, New England and Walton.

Finally, we trust this book will give as much pleasure as we have had in selecting the postcards, to evoke many happy memories for older residents, and for new residents, to show some of Peterborough's heritage and history.

June and Vernon Bull
May, 1988

THE CIVIC ARMS OF PETERBOROUGH

The old City Arms illustrated by a postcard published by Stoddart & Co. of Halifax in their 'Ja-Ja' heraldic series, which covered almost every city and town in the British Isles.

The old Arms were designed by the first Mayor, Mr. H.P. Gates, and the Rev. W.D. Sweeting, and adopted by the newly formed Municipal Corporation in 1874. The emblems on the shield represent the combination of the Arms of Joseph Henshaw, D.D., Bishop of Peterborough (1663-1679), shown on the left-hand side, and the Arms of James Dupont, D.D., Dean of Peterborough (1664-1679), shown on the right-hand side.

The City Arms have now been changed and were granted by Letters Patent on 6th September, 1960.

The new Arms consist of a shield with St. Peter's keys enfiled by a mural crown. Above the shield is the civic symbol of a larger mural crown with six towers. The shield is supported by two ermine lions with eagles' wings decorated by stars; derived from the lions of the Marquis of Exeter, heriditary Lord Paramount of Peterborough, and the eagles of Mordaunt, first Earl of Peterborough. The base consists of two tree trunks, derived from Earl Fitzwilliam's estate, and a slab of rock from its association with St. Peter. The motto beneath the shield is 'Upon this rock'.

PETERBOROUGH

HERALDIC SERIES.

1

he Lynch, Alwalton, near Peterborough   Do you know, I like this place

'ROMANTIC ALWALTON', c.1910

The winding route of the River Nene took its course through Alwalton Lynch on its way to the city centre. At the turn of the century it was a popular courting area.

The postcard was produced by superimposing the photograph of the couple over the view of the Lynch. The same couple were used for similar views all over the country!

S 1176   MILTON HALL, PETERBOROUGH.

MILTON HALL

Milton Hall was founded by the first Earl Fitzwilliam during the reign of King Henry VIII. It was rebuilt by Talman in 1688, who added the stabling court, Gibb in 1726, Brettingham in 1749, Fliterof in 1750-51, and the Tudor north front was re-roofed by Sir William Chambers in 1771.

The Hall has a Georgian west front and a late Elizabethan east front, which gives the appearance of a totally different building. The two-storied bay window, shown centre left on the postcard, dates from the mid-16th century.

Daphne Du Maurier, the authoress, refers to her visit to Milton Hall in 1917 in her biography, 'Growing Pains'. Also, 'Manderley', the home described in her novel 'Rebecca', was based on her childhood memories of Milton.

In the Great War, the Hall was used as a military hospital.

3

S 1148   THE HOUNDS, MILTON HALL. PETERBOROUGH.

MILTON HALL

The Milton Hall estate consists of the park, pleasure gardens, lake and boathouse, head gardener's home (formerly the Lodge), and the kennels for the Fitzwilliam hounds used for the many hunts.

The sixth Irish Earl (the fourth English Earl) Fitzwilliam, William Thomas Spencer Wentworth (1815-1902), inherited a colliery empire in South Yorkshire and the country estate of Wentworth Woodhouse which has 365 rooms. To this day the Fitzwilliam family spend half the year at Wentworth Woodhouse and the other half of the year at the magnificent Milton Hall, which is not open to the public.

MILTON NURSERIES, c.1916

Many of the extensive nursery buildings in Milton Park have now been demolished.

S 1161 LONGTHORPE, PETERBOROUGH.

LONGTHORPE, c.1910

A delightful view looking down Thorpe Road.

Longthorpe village, the site of an early Roman settlement, provides splendid examples of 17th and 18th century thatched cottages. The village was incorporated into the Municipal Borough of Peterborough in 1921.

6

LONGTHORPE, NEAR PETERBOROUGH

LONGTHORPE, c.1920

The original 'Fox and Hounds' public house situated on Thorpe Road. It burnt down on 6th January, 1928, and was later rebuilt as a two-storey building designed in mock-Tudor style. Sadly, the trees are no longer at the side of the road.

Peterborians used to take Christmas Eve walks to the 'Fox and Hounds' and then onto Midnight Mass at St. Botolph's Church, one of the oldest parish churches in the district.

THORPE PARK, c.1911

A group of children, possibly on a day's outing, photographed at one of the three entrances to Thorpe park, near the junction with Thorpe Road.

THORPE PARK, c.1911

Another view of the entrance to Thorpe Park, photographed further down the drive and looking back at the entrance lodge and a grocery delivery vehicle on its way to Thorpe Hall.

THORPE ROAD, c.1905

A horse-drawn bus on its way to Longthorpe Village and Castor, about to pass the old Toll House, now demolished and the site of one of the other entrances to Thorpe Hall.

S 1157   THORPE HALL, PETERBOROUGH

THORPE HALL, c.1914

Thorpe Hall was built between 1653 and 1656 for Oliver St. John, Lord Chief Justice, out of the ruins of the Bishop's Palace and Cloisters.

   The Rev. W. Strong, father of Colonel C.I. Strong (1838-1914), bought Thorpe Hall from the Fitzwilliams in the early 1860's.

   From 1939 to 1974, Thorpe Hall was owned by Peterborough District Hospital Board, and for part of this period it was a Maternity Hospital.

   The Hall has been recently acquired from the City Council by the Sue Ryder Foundation.

S 1154   THORPE ROAD, PETERBOROUGH

THORPE ROAD, c.1918

Looking down Thorpe Road towards Thorpe Hall, with the entrance to Westwood House on the right.

Peterborough, Sessions House, Thorpe Road.

THE SESSIONS-HOUSE, THORPE ROAD, c.1908

The Sessions-House, originally the prison and designed as a Norman castle, was completed in 1842.

In 1878, the prison was closed as the building proved to be inadequate for the ever increasing number of offenders; the prisoners being sent to either Cambridge or Northampton.

The building continued to serve as the Sessions-House until being replaced by the new Court House, built in Bridge Street in the mid-1960's. The site remained empty for nearly ten years and it is now occupied by a restaurant.

ALDERMAN'S DRIVE, PETERBOROUGH

99
COPYRIGHT

ALDERMANS DRIVE, c.1948

The roads leading off Alderman's Drive on the right-hand side were named after various city Aldermen: Percival, Clifton and Williamson.

Two houses in the left foreground, numbers 77 and 79, were demolished in the late 1960's to make way for the entrance to the new Peterborough Maternity Hospital.

New Bridge over G.N.R. Peterboro.

THE CRESCENT BRIDGE, 1913

The Crescent Bridge was opened on 16th April 1913 at a cost of £34,000. it was built to ease the traffic flow over the double crossing on the Great Northern Railway line.

The postcard was produced by J.F. Searle of Werrington and was posted by Albert who lived at 2, Orchard Street, Woodston.

G.N.R. STATION, PETERBOROUGH, c.1906

The main entrance to Peterborough North Railway Station and showing great activity with travellers arriving and departing. The horse-drawn carriages belonging to the Great Northern Hotel await to convey passengers to the city centre.

The station opened in August 1850 and was situated on the first direct route to London's Maiden Lane Station and also as the first important stopping place on the east coast route to the north.

On the left are a fine selection of G.N.R. advertisements giving details of rail travel to the continent and the east coast resorts of Whitby, Scarborough and Bridlington.

S 1156   PETERBOROUGH STATION, G.N. RAILWAY.

G.N.R. STATION, PETERBOROUGH, c.1911

The interior of the Great Northern Railway Station looking south towards London. The postcard shows a wide variety of enamel advertising boards featuring Allsopp's Pale Ale, Bovril, luxury cruises, G.N.R. travel to holiday resorts, and Stephen's ink.

Bookstalls and Refreshment Rooms are on both platforms and the footbridge connecting both sides can be seen in the centre of the picture.

M. R. SMASH PETERBOROUGH.

RAILWAY SMASH, 1922

On 14th August 1922, a runaway engine overran the buffers on the Midland Railway line, resulting in extensive damage to a house, and the engine just stopping short of the Crescent Bridge.

Note the picture, handbag and coat undamaged on the bedroom wall!

PETERBOROUGH INFIRMARY, c.1908

This building was built for Squire Cook in 1816. In 1856, it became the Dispensary and Infirmary given to the city by Earl Fitz-william in exchange for the city's premises in Milton Street.

Up until 1928 when the new War Memorial Hospital was completed, Peterborians paid 3d per week out of their pay towards hospital treatment.

This fine Georgian building is now occupied by the City Museum and Maxwell Art Gallery. It contains a unique collection of carved bonework and straw marquetry made by prisoners from the Napoleonic Wars held in Norman Cross Barracks.

COWGATE, PETERBOROUGH

47983

COWGATE, c.1916

Looking down Cowgate towards the Cathedral. On the left, the shops include: W.A. Rands 'Ye Olde Curiositie Shoppe', complete home furnisher and dealer in antiques; Charles Colls & Sons; and Alexander Thomson's department store, which had a covered walkway over King's Street linking their two stores. In the right foreground, the shops include: Rogers household stores; and Cash & Co., boots and shoes.

This photograph was taken shortly before Thomson's store was destroyed by fire towards the end of the Great War.

Cowgate, Peterborough

COWGATE

A close-up view of Rogers household stores, one of the city's best stocked stores where one could buy almost anything.

The windows and lighted display signs advertise glass, china, cutlery, cycles, lamps, plates and pop! Outside the shop, buckets, bowls and various bags and baskets complete the display.

In the centre foreground is a three-wheeled delivery cycle.

PETERBORO'—Baptist Chapel & Barrass Memorial Hall before the fire, Oct. 16, 1905.

QUEEN STREET, 1905

The Baptist Chapel and Barrass Memorial Hall opened on 26th May, 1904. Both buildings were very badly damaged by fire on 16th October, 1905. Thereafter, the Baptists moved to a new building in Park Road.

22

CHURCH STREET, c.1906

Showing the Corn Exchange in the left foreground, just before St. John's Parish Church. On the right-hand side of Church Street, the buildings include: the 'Vine' public house and the Tokio Tea Rooms. The entrance at the side of the 'Vine' led into Priestgate and gave access to the back gardens of the Tokio Tea Rooms.

Notice the horse-drawn taxis outside St. John's porch.

St. Johns Church, Peterborough

ST. JOHN'S CHURCH, CHURCH STREET, 1905

St. John's Parish Church was built in 1407. At the beginning of the nineteenth century, the Church tower possessed a spire which caused great concern because of its ruinous condition, eventually it was taken down some years later.

One of the unusual features of the Church was the storage of the city fire engines in the west end up until 1871.

In the left foreground is the mobile tea room of the horse-drawn taxi-cab drivers, and in the right foreground is the hand-operated water-pump used by the fish stall-holders on market days.

PETERBOROUGH FROM ST. JOHN'S CHURCH, c.1920

A view of Market Place on market day photographed from the tower of St. John's Church.

In the foreground the buildings include: the 'Greyhound' public house; the rating offices; and the old Town Hall. On the corner of Long Causeway are Market Chambers and Gill's China Stores.

The triple-arched West Front of the Cathedral, flanked by pinnacled towers, and described as 'the magnificent portico in Christendom' was built in the early 13th century. Each of the gothic-styled arches are 85 feet high, and the porch below the centre arch was added in c.1370.

THE GUILDHALL, CATHEDRAL SQUARE, c.1905

The Guildhall was completed in 1671 and used as the Town Hall and Council Chamber between 1874 and 1933.

    The photograph also shows the old Police Station in between St. John's Church and the Town Hall, and on the right, the old rating offices. Both buildings have now been demolished.

THE PROCLAMATION OF H.M. KING GEORGE V

A rare postcard showing the Proclamation of H.M. King George V by the Mayor outside the Town Hall on 12th May 1910. A specially constructed podium holds the invited audience of church and civic dignitaries, and within the square surrounded by the military guard-of-honour are members of the City Fire Service, choristers and three buglers.

In the background are the 'Bell and Oak' and 'Greyhound' public houses.

THE MARKET PLACE, PETERBOROUGH.

MARKET PLACE, c.1909

Market Place was the terminal point for trams after their journey along Long Causeway.

The postcard shows from left to right: Wrigley & Sons Ltd., clothiers; the 12th century St. Nicholas' Gate; George C. Caster, printer, bookseller and stationer; The London Clothing Company's Depot with a Railway collecting van outside; and on the far right, the premises belonging to House Furnishers and Removal Contractors.

MARKET PLACE c,1917

A later view of the premises in Market Place and showing considerable alterations to the buildings on the left of St. Nicholas' Gate.

On the far left, the shops occupied by I. & S. Crane and Amies & Son have a new facade; next door, Wrigley's the clothiers have become the Canadian emigration office (later to become Gill's China Stores — see page 25); and on the corner, the new gothic-styled Lloyd's Bank.

The tram advertises Hudson's and Nubolic soaps, and A.J. Robert & Son, outfitters.

PETERBORO' GRAMMAR SCHOOL

KING'S GRAMMAR SCHOOL, c.1904

In 1854, King's Grammar School was situated in the Cathedral Precincts. Extra teaching space and accommodation were provided by adjacent houses, the room above St. Nicholas' Gate and the Thomas à Becket Chapel, shown on the right.

In 1905, the Thomas à Becket Chapel was used for the Peterborough Museum.

THE KING'S LODGING, c.1908

The King's Lodging in the Cathedral yard when it was occupied by a chemist and druggist.

ETCHES & HALL,
COPYRIGHT.

TROOPS IN PETERBOROUGH.-CHURCH PARADE.

CHURCH PARADE

Soldiers of the Terratorial Army marching to their first Sunday Service held in the Cathedral in March 1915. Prior to this date, the Service had been held in St. John's Parish Church.

Peterborough Cathedral and Bishops Palace

Made by WH Berlin 3146

PETERBOROUGH CATHEDRAL, c.1903

The first church was founded by Peada, King of Mercia, in 655 A.D., and later destroyed by the Danes in 870 A.D. The second church was built by King Edgar and completed by 972 A.D., but was destroyed by fire in 1116. The present building of local Barnack stone and a superb example of Norman-Romanesque architecture was begun in 1118 by Abbot Jean de Seez and finally consecrated in c.1238. During the Reformation, Henry VIII preserved the church and elevated its status to a cathedral in 1541. It was badly damaged during the Civil War but fragments of the mediaeval glass were preserved and can be seen in the Apse, beyond the Sanctuary.

At the end of the nineteenth century, the Central Tower was completely rebuilt and the Bishop's Throne and the High Altar were added. The postcard illustrated is known as a 'hold-to-light' card. The moon and a selection of windows have been cut out, backed with thin card, and will appear to light up when held to sunlight.

Peterborough Cathedral.

Valentine's Series

PETERBOROUGH CATHEDRAL, c.1905

A south-east view of the Cathedral church dedicated to St. Peter, St. Paul and St. Andrew, and showing the Eastern Building, behind the Central Tower, added between 1496 and 1508 with Perpendicular fan vaulting designed by John Wastell.

The Cathedral has numerous features including the unique painted wooden ceiling (c.1220), a rare brass Eagle Lectern, the tomb of Katherine of Aragon, the former burial place of Mary, Queen of Scots, the Hedda Stone (c.780), and the painted ceiling by Sir George Gilbert Scott in the Apse.

In the late 19th century, the surrounding fields were rented from the Ecclesiastical Commissioners by Gaunts the butchers, Westgate, for grazing.

Peterboro' College.

The Wrench Series, No. 6097

ST. PETER'S COLLEGE, CITY ROAD

In 1850 the Diocese of Peterborough decided to build a teacher training college and by 1859, the red and blue brick building called St. Peter's College was completed.

It was used as a male teacher training college until it closed in 1914. It re-opened in 1921 as a women's teacher training college but sadly it closed in the mid 1930's.

The gothic-style building, known as Peterscourt, is now used as offices.

BISHOPS ROAD GARDENS, c.1907

The gardens are situated south of the Minster Precincts. In the centre of the picture is St. Oswald's House built by the Thompson family, who founded the Florence Saunders Nursing Home.

PETERBOROUGH CATHEDRAL ENTRANCE TO DEANERY

32544

ENTRANCE TO DEANERY, c.1925

In 1496 Robert Kirkton succeeded Abbot Ramsey. In c.1508 Abbot Kirkton was fined £20 for poaching so he decided to create his own park and built this ornate gateway as the entrance. His hieroglyphic signature can be seen over the archway.

Abbot Kirkton also had an apartment built in the Bishop's Palace called Heaven's Gate or Chamber.

LAUREL COURT, c.1912

Laurel Court is an early 18th century home situated on the north side of the Cathedral. It was once used as a school where Edith Cavell taught for some time in the late 19th century.

THE BROADWAY, PETERBOROUGH.

BROADWAY, c.1908

Looking down Broadway and showing the entertainment centres of Peterborough. On the left is the Broadway Kinema featuring the 'well known' film 'Her Vengeance': the Kinema has now become a bingo hall. On the right is Mear's Tea and Refreshment Rooms and the 'Hippodrome' music hall which opened on 16th September, 1907. The theatre was owned by a London syndicate managed by Mr. T. Sylvester, and in 1908, the 'Hippodrome' changed ownership to the famous theatrical troupe owner, Fred Karno. Many leading music hall stars appeared at the 'Hippodrome' including Veron Watson, Marie Lloyd and Charlie Chaplin.

In 1924, the lease of the 'Hippodrome' was taken on by Mr. Jack Bancroft, who subsequently purchased the building in 1930 and renamed it the 'Palace'. In 1937, Mr. Bancroft built the Embassy Cinema next door and the 'Palace' was later demolished.

THE THEATRE ROYAL

An advertisement card for Peterborough Boys Brigade who performed 'Cricket on the Hearth' at the Theatre Royal on Thursday, 18th January, 1906. Bookings were obtainable from Messrs. Claypole and Sons, Narrow Bridge Street.

The Theatre Royal was designed by the London architects, Pye and Hayward, and built in 1877 originally as a public hall with its main entrance facing Park Road. It was converted to the Theare Royal in 1894 and later changed its name to the 'Grand' in April, 1916. The 'Grand' closed in c.1957 and the site is now occupied by Shelton's department store.

GRAND THEATRE
PETERBOROUGH

EXTRAORDINARY ATTRACTION

FOR SIX NIGHTS commencing

MONDAY, OCT. 29th, 1917

MATINEE - SATURDAY at 2.30

W. W. KELLY'S LONDON COMPANY
IN THE PLAY OF TWO CENTURIES

A Royal Divorce

A Story of Waterloo   By W. G. Wills

This Play has toured continuously for over 26 Years
and during that period has played 66 engage-
ments in both Liverpool and Manchester thereby
constituting an absolute record

Miss **MABEL SCUDAMORE** as Josephine

Mr. **GEORGE HUDSON** as Napoleon

Popular Prices.   Book Your Seats at once

Photo by "Daily Mirror

POST CARD

THE ADDRESS ONLY TO BE
WRITTEN HERE

AFFIX
HALFPENNY
STAMP

NOTICE.

From **MONDAY, OCTOBER 29th**
and during the Winter Season, the
Performances at this Theatre will
begin at **7-15**; doors open at **6-30**.

There will be **NO Early Doors.**

*First Come—First Served
with Seats.*

Seats may be booked at Box
Office, or by **Telephone 223.**

Matinees Wednesday & Saturday
at 2-30.

GRAND THEATRE, 1917

An early advertising postcard for the Grand Theatre, Broadway, giving details of 'A Royal Divorce' — a story of Waterloo.
This touring production visited most of the major provincial theatres around the country.

Arcadian Follies, Peterborough, 1932.

THE ARCADIAN FOLLIES, 1932

The 1932 Arcadian Follies troupe who appeared regularly at the Grand Theatre, Peterborough.

Among the members of the cast identified are: Edith Alderman, stage name — Ena Roscoe (centre of back row); Maisie Norris (fourth from right, back row); Harry Korris (middle of centre row); Albert Modley (second right, centre row), and Max Norris (far right, centre row).

Edith Alderman, Harry Korris and Albert Modley all performed on BBC Radio during the 1930s.

Public Library, Peterborough.

THE PUBLIC LIBRARY, BROADWAY, 1915

The Public Library was opened in 1906 at a cost of more than £6,000 donated by Mr. Andrew Carnegie, the famous Scottish-American millionaire and Freeman of the City of Peterborough.

When this picture was taken, the Head Librarian was W.J. Willcock.

The Broadway, Peterborough.

BROADWAY, c.1907

Looking down Broadway with the junction of Church Walk in the left foreground and showing a solitary horse and cart in the distance.
The large tree in the centre marks the junction of Lincoln Road East (now Burghley Road).

New Road and Council Schools, Peterborough.

COUNCIL SCHOOLS, NEW ROAD, c.1904

The Council School produced one of the city's greatest school masters, Benjamin Dennison, known affectionately by his pupils as 'Daddy Dennison' and who retired after more than 40 years service in July, 1905.

At one time, non-conformist parents living in New England would send their children walking to the school, rather than let them attend one of the nearer Church of England schools.

The site is now occupied by T.C. Harrison Ltd., Ford motor dealer.

ST. MARY'S CHURCH, NEW ROAD, c.1905

The Parish of St. Mary was created by Council order on 1st September, 1857. The Church was built on a site given by the Hon. George Wentworth Fitzwilliam and the first stone was laid by Bishop Magee on 30th May, 1859.

In the left foreground, the tram is proceeding towards Market Place. The advertisement above the driver's cab reads 'This car stops at C.W. Allen's, Long Causeway'.

Eastfield Road, Peterborough.

EASTFIELD ROAD, c.1905

Photographed from near the junctions of Monument Street and Whalley Street.

    Showing the iron railings of the City Cemetery on the left, and on the right, the entrance to Padholme Road and Stephens memorials, now owned by G.R. Dickens & Son, Ltd., memorial masons.

NEWARK VILLAGE, PETERBOROUGH

NEWARK VILLAGE, c.1905

A rural scene showing a one storey thatched cottage built in the early 18th century on the left, and on the right, the 'Royal Arms' public house and the main road leading back to the centre of Peterborough.

This area is now part of Eastfield and is virtually unrecognisable today.

NEWARK VILLAGE, c.1920

A close-up of the 'Royal Arms' public house on Newark Road. At the time, it was managed by George H. Turner and sold ales and stouts brewed by Elgoods of Wisbech.

The 'Royal Arms' has now been demolished.

STANGROUND

The last week of August 1912 was reported as 'this black week of rack and ruin'. Heavy rain caused Stanground Lode to rise and the road from High Street to Peterborough was covered in places by up to four feet of water (see also page 53).

This rare postcard shows the Green at Stanground covered by over one foot of water and in the left background, can be seen the Urban Council dray utilised to ferry pedestrians and cyclists across the flooded area. (Church Street is to the left and South Street to the right.)

High Street, Old Fletton

HIGH STREET, FLETTON, c.1925

This view looking towards Stanground shows little change today. On the left, the picture shows a small fish and chip hut, the corner of Duke Street, and a small parade of shops including H. Edis, grocers.

Fletton Avenue, Peterborough.

FLETTON AVENUE, c.1909

Looking back towards Fletton with a horse and cart carrying peas to Farrow's pea factory, which is obscured by trees on the right-hand side.

OUNDLE R^D PETERBOROUGH IN FLOOD. AUG 1912.

OUNDLE ROAD, 1912

A further view of the flooding caused by heavy rain in August 1912 and photographed at the junction with London Road and Oundle Road, looking towards Woodston village.

Notice the planks constructed as walkways under the railway bridge to allow pedestrians and cyclists to pass freely. The flood water appears to be about two feet deep in the centre of the road.

LONDON RD PETERBORO . 227.

LONDON ROAD, c.1912

A superb and very collectable postcard showing the Great Eastern Railway crossing, London Road.
A wealth of detail can be seen in the centre with a wide variety of transport making their way to and from the city centre.
On the right is the wooden footbridge serving the G.E.R. Station and the two shops are occupied by Goodson, grocers, and Pacey, cycle dealers. The advertisements include Quaker oats, Pedley tyres, Imperial cycles and Vulcanizing by Harvey Frost.

Town Bridge.
No. 12372 *Compliments of the Season, 1904* *Peterborough.*

TOWN BRIDGE, c.1904

The River Nene and Town Bridge looking eastwards towards Whittlesey. On the left is H.W. Elderkin's tobacco kiosk and the Central Temperance Hotel and Restaurant, which offered good accommodation for commercial travellers and cyclists. On the right is the Midland Railway Company's Number One grain warehouse. Notice the horse-drawn bus crossing the bridge.

TOWN BRIDGE, c.1906

The opposite side of Town Bridge looking westwards towards Woodston. The photograph shows the Midland Railway Number Two grain warehouse on the left, and on the right, the Customs House and the moorings for the river barges and pleasure boats.

The River Nene, Peterborough.

THE RIVER NENE, c.1930

Hiring pleasure boats and taking trips along the River Nene has always been a popular pastime with Peterborians. At night, the boats would be secured and the oars and sails locked away in the houseboat, shown on the right.

This part of the riverbank is now the site of the Key Theatre.

Town Bridge and Bridge Street, Peterborough.

TOWN BRIDGE AND BROAD BRIDGE STREET, c.1907

Looking down Broad Bridge Street and probably photographed from a barge moored on the River Nene. Town Bridge was opened in 1872 and constructed by a Derby firm for the price of £5,246.

On the left is the Boat Inn, and today all the buildings, with the exception of their frontage, have been demolished. On the right-hand side of the street, the new buildings today include the Magistrate's Court, the Police Station and a small parade of shops.

BROAD BRIDGE STREET, c.1906

Two cows passing the old 'Saracen's Head' public house on their way to Cow Pastures Farm, Woodston. How times have changed!
Older residents may remember Mrs. Hankey's fish shop and Reed's barber shop.
The Golden Lion Commercial Hotel can be seen in the left background.

BROAD BRIDGE STREET, c.1912

A close-up view of the end of Broad Bridge Street and showing the entrance to Narrow Bridge Street to the left of the Golden Lion Hotel.

On the extreme right, notice the men attending to the old gas lamp on the corner of Bishops Road.

The Golden Lion Hotel was demolished in the late 1920's to make way for the new Town Hall.

BROAD BRIDGE STREET, 1911

Photographed from the first floor of the Golden Lion Hotel and showing the vast crowds lining Broad Bridge Street on the occasion of the Coronation celebrations for Their Majesties King George V and Queen Mary on 22nd June, 1911.

A splendid steam traction-engine hauling a 'Royal' float can be seen about to enter Narrow Bridge Street. Numerous other floats are lined up behind ready to complete the procession.

In the far distance are Fletton brickyards.

S 1169. NARROW BRIDGE STREET, PETERBOROUGH.

NARROW BRIDGE STREET, c.1905

Looking down Narrow Bridge Street from the corner of Priestgate. On the left the shops include: E.A. Hooke, bookseller and stationer; and Freeman, Hardy and Willis.

The Angel Hotel, shown in the right foreground, was an inn for nearly 500 years. In the 15th century the building belonged to the Abbey, and later in the 18th century the Angel became an important coaching inn. One of the landlords during the height of the coaching era was Alderman Joseph Clifton. Before the motor age, the 'Angel' boasted the finest wedding turn-out and many local girls booked their horse and trap from there. The Angel Hotel was demolished in 1972.

Peterborough : Narrow Bridge Street.

NARROW BRIDGE STREET, c.1907

Photographed from the corner of Market Place (Cathedral Square) and showing the top end of Narrow Bridge Street.

The shops in the left foreground include: Pearson's, chemist and druggist; and next door, a tobacconist and confectioner. Scales and Sons' boot and shoe shop can be seen in the distance on the right-hand side of the street.

In the right foreground, the Midland Bank, one of the largest constructed buildings of its time, caused great controversy when it was built in 1902, as the proposed widening of Narrow Bridge Street was to take place by utilising the site on which the bank was eventually built.

Market Place, Peterborough

MARKET PLACE, c.1912

The fountain and monument was erected in 1898 in memory of the first mayor of the city, Henry Pearson Gates (1818-1893), who was mayor in 1875, 1876 and 1887, and who donated the mace to the city. The Gates' monument stood in the centre of Market Place and was later moved, without its plinth, granite basins and taps, to Bishop's Gardens in 1963.

Bordering Market Place, the premises included: The Carpet Warehouse; Howe's, gentlemen's outfitters; Claributt's, ladies' outfitters; a funeral director; and to the left of the Town Hall, the newly-constructed Stamford, Spalding and Boston Bank, later to become Barclays Bank,.

The small arch behind the Gates' monument led to May Bones, photographer. The block of buildings between the monument and the bank were later redesigned and housed the Dujon Café and Restaurant and Boots the Chemist (see cover illustration).

32593. PETERBOROUGH: MARKET PLACE.

MARKET PLACE, c.1904

The old Wednesday market was held in Peterborough from the Middle Ages up to the early 1960's. The market area was sometimes referred to as the Butter Cross because until the late 1920's, Fen women used to sell butter, eggs and poultry on this site.

The two buildings on the right of the Town Hall were occupied by city council offices, which included the Rating Department, and Robert Back, a watchmaker. Both buildings were demolished in May, 1923.

The postcard was published by George Caster, bookseller and stationer, and photographed from the second-floor of his building next to St. Nicholas' Gate.

Town Hall. St. Johns Church and Market Place, Peterborough

MARKET PLACE, c.1925

Photographed after the demolition of the old city council offices and showing the newly-constructed Boots the Chemist on the extreme left, and on the right, Exchange Street and part of the Corn Exchange at the rear of St. John's Church.

LONG CAUSEWAY, c.1912

Looking down Long Causeway to Barrett's Corner with a Walton tram returning to the tram terminus.

On the left the premises include: Willson, chemist; Brainsby & Sons, leading carriage and buggy makers; Duddington's toy shop; on the corner of Cumbergate, the Trustee Savings Bank; and beyond, Neaverson, fruiterer and confectioner.

67

LONG CAUSEWAY, c.1906

A very collectable postcard illustrating Neaverson's staff and shop front at 18, Long Causeway. The splendid window displays show fruit and confectionery on the left and right sides respectively, and the entrance floor by the door advertises the message 'The Popular Top Tea Shop'.

Neaverson's had two other shops at 38, Broad Bridge Street and Bridge End.

HAVE YOU SEEN

JAPAN in

PETERBORO'?

Ices & Iced Drinks

are being served in a

lovely cool Japanese

Garden at . . .

NEAVERSON'S

18 Long Causeway

Peterborough.

⇢ **TEAS & LIGHT REFRESHMENTS.** ⇠
COOLEST PLACE IN THE CITY—COOLED BY ELECTRICITY.

LONG CAUSEWAY

How many Peterborians remember taking tea in Neaverson's cool Japanese Garden?
An early advertising card produced for Neaversons. Notice the sub-heading: 'Coolest place in the city — cooled by electricity'.

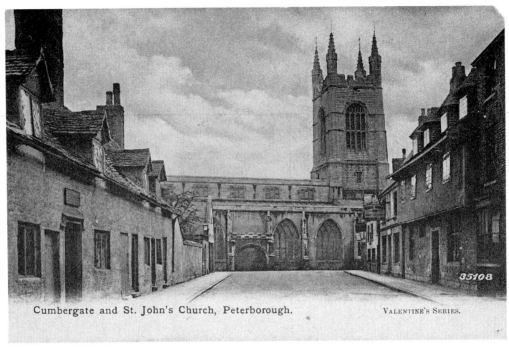

Cumbergate and St. John's Church, Peterborough.

VALENTINE'S SERIES.

35108

CUMBERGATE, c.1902

A view of Cumbergate leading to its junction with Exchange Street. On the left-hand side are the Almshouses and the old Bridewell or House of Correction, which the various town charities maintained for minor offenders. Towards the end of Cumbergate, on the right, are the White Horse Inn and the 'Coach and Horses' public house.

70

CUMBERGATE, c.1905

A later view showing changes to the left-hand side of Cumbergate after demolition of the row of the old Almshouses had taken place, and replaced by Miss Pear's Almshouses built in c.1903. The Almshouses were named after Miss Frances Pears, the daughter of a Peterborough draper, who left a legacy of £5,000. The building is now used as an Italian restaurant.

Peterboro. General Post Office.

CUMBERGATE, 1906

The General Post Office was built in 1874 and extended in 1904. The postcard was posted in 1906, the same year that horse-drawn vans were beginning to be replaced by motor transport.

Notice the line of seven postmen photographed before their delivery round — how times have changed!

LONG CAUSEWAY, PETERBOROUGH

LONG CAUSEWAY, c.1906

Looking back towards Market Place and showing the Trustee Savings Bank and the corner of Cumbergate in more detail.
The tram driver is turning the pole on the tram, ready for its departure and outward journey to Newark village.

Long Causeway, Peterborough

Valentines Series

LONG CAUSEWAY, c.1906

The junction of Long Causeway and Midgate was popularly known as Barrett's Corner, after T.L. Barrett's department store which stood on the corner site.

Plenty of activity is in evidence along the busy thoroughfare. Notice the policeman on duty in the foreground and keeping an eye on the photographer. The Borough Constabulary was at one time known as the Liberty Force.

Also in the centre foreground can be seen the intersection of the tram routes to Midgate and New Road on the left and Westgate on the right.

Long Causeway, Peterborough

JV 80334

LONG CAUSEWAY, c.1914

A final view of Long Causeway and showing the shops on the right-hand side in greater detail. The shops from right to left are: Freeman, Hardy and Willis; Paten and Co., wine and spirit merchants, with a number of their barrels standing in the road; and two shops further on, Neaverson's, recognisable by the long vertical Restaurant sign above the roof. Beyond, in the centre of the photograph, the tallest building is the Trustee Savings Bank.

PETERBOROUGH PEACE CELEBRATIONS, 1919

Photographed at the end of Broadway, near the junctions of Midgate, Long Causeway and Westgate.
The postcard is one of a long series depicting the Peterborough Peace Celebrations held in July, 1919.
In the background, the nearest premises belong to Webster and Abington and Sons.

MANSION HOUSE AND WESTGATE, PETERBOROUGH.

J. W. Bodger, Peterborough and Hunstanton.

WESTGATE. 1903

Looking down Westgate and photographed at its junction with Long Causeway. The Mansion House, shown on the right of the picture, was built during the mid-18th century by Matthew Wyldbore (1722-1787). Born in Peterborough and finishing his education at Trinity College, Cambridge, he represented Peterborough as its M.P. in two successive Parliaments.

WESTGATE, PETERBOROUGH.

WESTGATE, c.1908

Showing the new parade of shops built next to the Mansion House in c.1905 (compare previous page).
The Mansion House was later demolished in 1925/26.

A.A. APPOINTED   BULL HOTEL, PETERBOROUGH   R.A.C. APPOINTED

THE FINE NEW WING WITH 22 ROOMS FITTED WITH HOT AND COLD WATER
AND GAS FIRES CAN BE SEEN ON THE EXTREME RIGHT OF THE PHOTOGRAPH

THE BULL HOTEL, WESTGATE, c.1928

The Bull Hotel has been a well-known hostelry since the Coaching Age. Its frontage dates from the late 18th century, and in 1900, alterations were made to the roof to accommodate a second-storey and extra bedrooms.

The postcard shows the hotel's new wing with 22 rooms, and the three shops at street level, which were built on the site of the former Mansion House after 1926.

Westgate, Peterborough

Valentines Series

WESTGATE, c.1902

A view of Westgate before the double tram lines were laid and looking towards Barrett's Corner.
In the left foreground is Taylor & Downs, stationer and newsagents; and in the right foreground, Walter Bisele's general store.

WESTGATE, c.1904

Photographed from Bisele's store and showing the parade of shops on the opposite side of Westgate.

The junction of North Street can be seen on the extreme left, and J.H. Duddington, wholesale and retail ironmongers, haberdashers, hosiers and stationers, in the right foreground.

WESTGATE. PETERBOROUGH.

WESTGATE, c.1927

Looking down Westgate towards the Cathedral, and photographed between the junctions of North Street and Boroughbury Road.

The postcard shows a wealth of detail which includes from left to right: J.W. Morton, greengrocery, behind the lamp-post; an outward tram (possibly bound for Walton) advertising Claypole's; the garage on the corner with Queen Street; and the Royal Hotel, dating back to the late 18th century, and advertising Allsopp's Pale and Burton Ales.

Does anybody remember owning an Austin Seven, reg. no. UT 331, or a motor-cycle, reg. no. FL 6060? Both vehicles are shown in the right foreground.

82

WESTGATE, SHOWING WESTGATE CHURCH, PETERBOROUGH.

WESTGATE, c.1914

A final view of Westgate from the Royal Hotel and looking back towards the Congregational Church. Westgate and Long Causeway were the only streets which had double tramlines and this postcard clearly shows the tracks turning right into Boroughbury Road, where they became a single track.

In the centre can be seen the underground public conveniences, and to the right, Hubbard's newsagents, and a Walton Tram returning to Long Causeway.

AN ELECTRIC TRAM, c.1918

Succeeding the horse-buses, the electric tramways were introduced in 1903 and operated for twenty-seven years.

This superb postcard illustrates one of the city trams on its way back to the Lincoln Road depot. The advertisement reads, 'All cars stop at 'Farrow's Corner' — the most up to date Drapers in the City'. (Farrow's Corner was located on the corner of Westgate and Broadway and is now Courts Furnishers).

Peterborough Co-operative Stores, Park Road.

PARK ROAD, c.1906

A locally produced postcard by Taylor and Downs, Westgate, and showing the Co-operative Society Stores; photographed at the beginning of Park Road at its junction with Westgate. This fine building also possessed a dance hall on its first floor.

S 1150　　　　PARK ROAD & BAPTIST CHAPEL, PETERBOROUGH.

PARK ROAD, c.1910

Looking back towards Westgate with the Co-operative stores in the centre background. The Baptist Church, on the corner of Geneva Street and on the right of the picture, was built on land purchased from Alderman Nichols and Mrs Heanley for £2,174. The church was built by Mr. J. Cracknell of Huntly Grove for £7,090. It was completed in 1907 and the opening ceremony was performed by Mrs Knee.

Fitzwilliam Street, Peterborough.

FITZWILLIAM STREET, c.1906

Photographed from near the junction of Lincoln Road and looking towards the junction with Park Road, and Broadway in the far distance.

On the right can be seen All Souls' Church, which was built on land acquired for £2,000 in 1883. The foundation stone of the present Church was laid in 1895 by the Bishop of Northampton and the building was completed in 1896.

Park Road, Peterborough.

PARK ROAD, c.1906

Not a vehicle in sight!
   Published by Taylor and Downs and looking down Park Road by the junction with Manor House Street. A number of notable families lived along this road.

KING'S SCHOOL, PARK ROAD, PETERBOROUGH.

KING'S SCHOOL, PARK ROAD, c.1917

The King's School moved from the Cathedral Precincts in 1885 to new buildings and its present position in Park Road.

The school stands on a four acre site which was obtained in exchange for land in Thorpe Road, opposite the Memorial Hospital, and owned by the Dean and Chapter. The school laboratories were provided by Mr. W.E. Cross, headmaster from 1909 to 1913, who was responsible for introducing science as part of the school curriculum.

The King's School, Peterborough.
The Manual Room.

KING'S SCHOOL, PARK ROAD

Before the 20th century, the school day at King's started at 7 a.m. and most of the time was devoted to Latin and Greek studies.

The school was maintained by fees and endowments up until 1905 when public money first became available. The school became co-educational in September, 1976.

This early postcard, possibly produced for school use, shows the Manual Room.

THE GIRLS' HIGH SCHOOL, PARK ROAD, c.1908

In 1907, the Girls' High School moved to Park Road to the building shown above which had formerly been a public library. The school moved to Westwood House on Thorpe Road in c.1938.

The building in Park Road was later used as the headquarters for the Post Office Engineering Staff, and today, the site is now occupied by a modern block of apartments.

The junction on the right leads to Huntly Grove.

BANDSTAND, THE PARK, PETERBOROUGH

THE PARK, c.1920

In the late 1880's, the Park was laid out by the Peterborough Land Company.

This delightful postcard shows the avenue leading to the bandstand, where various brass bands played every Thursday and Sunday evening during the summer months. The bandstand has now been demolished.

Deacon's School used to hold the lease on the cricket and football pitches.

CROMWELL ROAD, c.1910

Photograhed at the intersection with Russell Street. The 'Steam Engine' public house is just out of view on the left, and on the right, Grantham's corner shop and Seegow's fish shop beyond, with the flag pole outside.

LINCOLN ROAD, PETERBOROUGH

Published by W. H. Pentney, Peterborough

LINCOLN ROAD, c.1906

A view of Lincoln Road and the spire of St. Mark's Church photographed from the junction of St. Mark's Street.

The foundation stone for St. Mark's Church was laid by the Bishop of Peterborough in August, 1855. The first service was held in November, 1856 and in 1858, St. Mark's became a separate parish.

The tram, shown on the right, is on its way to Walton.

S 5903　　　　　　　　LIME TREE AVENUE, PETERBOROUGH.

LIME TREE AVENUE, c.1911
Showing some of the splendid late Victorian houses which exist in Lime Tree Avenue. This view is little changed today.

GLADSTONE STREET, c.1909

Looking up Gladstone Street (formerly Spring Hill) from the junction with Taverner's Road. On the left is the Gladstone Street sub-post office, and on the right, the small building is part of St. Barnabas' Church buildings.

LINCOLN ROAD, c.1907

A view of Lincoln Road looking towards Millfield. The 'Norfolk' public house and the junction with Dogsthorpe Road can be seen in the distance, in the centre of the picture.

Apart from the removal of the tram lines, which continued on to Walton, the buildings shown have changed very little over the years.

DOGSTHORPE ROAD, c.1913

Looking towards Dogsthorpe and photographed near the junctions of Green Lane on the left and Huntly Grove on the right.
The building on the corner of Green Lane has been demolished to make way for warden-controlled flats for the elderly. At the time the picture was taken, the corner shop on the right belonged to J. Lord, grocer and tea dealer. Notice the old 'Brasso' advertisement above the entrance.

PETERBOROUGH. MILLFIELD. LINCOLN ROAD.

LINCOLN ROAD, MILLFIELD, c.1907

Millfield Mill, or known locally as Adam's Mill, with its six wind-sails was demolished in 1937. The windmill gave its name to Windmill Street and Adams' Garage was built on its site.

The view has been photographed near the junction with St. Martin's Street.

NEW ENGLAND. The Fountain

LINCOLN ROAD, NEW ENGLAND, c.1906

New England was the site of the first major expansion plan in the city. The Great Northern Railway established locomotive works at New England in 1853. During the next six years up to 1869, it became a small railway town with its own church, chapel, school, shops and three public houses.

On the right, in the foreground, the drinking fountain was built c.1860, and behind, is the 'Locomotive' public house.

100

Dogsthorpe Village.

DOGSTHORPE VILLAGE, c.1908

A view of the centre of Dogsthorpe; photographed in Welland Road looking towards St. Paul's Road with the junction of Dogsthorpe Road on the left.

The rural scene is virtually unrecognisable today, the three 17th century cottages have been demolished. One of the sites was occupied by Meadows, bakers.

Paston Church, near Peterborough.

ALL SAINTS' CHURCH, PASTON, c.1910

The Parish Church of All Saints built with Barnack rag stone and dating back to the 11th century, has undergone many restorations over the years.

In 1884, the nave and aisle were restored at a cost of £1,000. In 1876, the Rev. Joseph Pratt was so popular that his fame as a preacher caused Paston Church to become overcrowded. To accommodate the increased congregation, a gallery was built at the west end of the Church. In 1901/1902, the chancel was rebuilt, and in 1929, the Church tower and spire were restored. During this work, large stones were discovered and identified as perfect coffins of Barnack rag stone — it is believed that these were built into the tower in 1260.

Recent work has included the north aisle being re-roofed in 1938 and a vestry built in the early 1950's.

WALTON, c.1906

The tram terminus in Walton was situated in Walton Road (now part of Lincoln Road).

The house on the left belonged to Mrs. Johnston, where tea and a bun could be purchased for 1d. She also served as the collection depot for parcels delivered by tram.

In those days, the cost of travelling by tram (single fare) from Walton to the Lincoln Road depot and Market Place was 1d and 2d respectively.

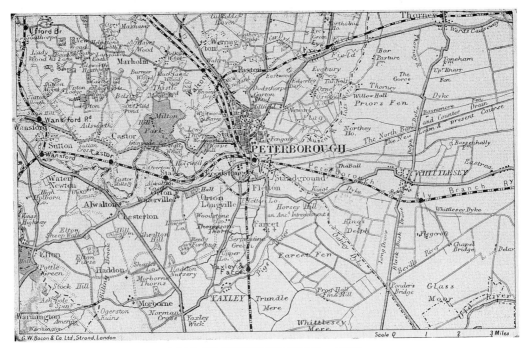

MAP OF PETERBOROUGH, c.1910

Scale: one inch represents approximately three miles.